I decree and declare generational wealth for you and your family.

BUILDING GENERATIONAL WEALTH

For Your Children's Children

MARY AYISI BOADU

authorHOUSE

AuthorHouse™ UK
1663 Liberty Drive
Bloomington, IN 47403 USA
www.authorhouse.co.uk
Phone: UK TFN: 0800 0148641 (Toll Free inside the UK)
UK Local: (02) 0369 56322 (+44 20 3695 6322 from outside the UK)

© 2022 Mary Ayisi Boadu. All rights reserved.

No part of this book may be reproduced, stored in a retrieval system, or transmitted by any means without the written permission of the author.

Published by AuthorHouse 11/30/2022

ISBN: 978-1-7283-7934-0 (sc)
ISBN: 978-1-7283-7692-9 (e)

Print information available on the last page.

Any people depicted in stock imagery provided by Getty Images are models, and such images are being used for illustrative purposes only. Certain stock imagery © Getty Images.

This book is printed on acid-free paper.

Because of the dynamic nature of the Internet, any web addresses or links contained in this book may have changed since publication and may no longer be valid. The views expressed in this work are solely those of the author and do not necessarily reflect the views of the publisher, and the publisher hereby disclaims any responsibility for them.

Scripture quotations are from the Holy Bible, King James Version (Authorized Version). First published in 1611. Quoted from the KJV Classic Reference Bible, Copyright © 1983 by The Zondervan Corporation.

Dedication

This book is dedicated to my mother, Mrs Augustina Ayisi, who passed on to eternity.

If I were to look up 'gift from God' in the dictionary, your picture would be there. Throughout your life, you thought and planned for your generations born and unborn. Everything you did had your children's children in mind. You used to speak of 'generations' when we had no clue about the meaning of that word until you passed on.

You have empowered and given us stability with so many options. Indeed, you changed our family tree, and we are grateful. I therefore dedicate this book to you.

Acknowledgements

Writing a book is not an individual project but takes an entire team. Especially on a subject such as building generational wealth, you involve your children. Therefore, I would like to give credit to my children, Nicole, Kelly-Louise, and Mikayla, for buying into my calling and understanding the message I carry to them, their children, their children's children, and our future generations.

My mother who has been called to heaven, Mrs Augustina Ayisi, embedded the words 'generational wealth' into us. She gave us everything any child could ever ask for, and it did not stop there. She created businesses and taught us practical ways to build businesses. She was always thinking about her great-grand kids. I wish she was still here with us, but our Lord knows best. Her name will forever live on, and may her soul rest in peace.

All thanks also to my husband, Nick, for the support and finally understanding my calling to help people avoid debt to build generational wealth.

Preface

When we talk about wealth, we're not talking about riches, so please do not get it wrong. What we're talking about is financial independence. When people are in debt, they develop stress and anxiety, and these can lead to sicknesses and diseases such as high blood pressure, heart attack, depression, insomnia, constipation and other bowel issues, diabetes, and cancer. It makes you wonder why people overspend and what we spend our money on.

The cause of the overspending could be that we are too materialistic, excessively concerned about material possessions we don't even need. Most people are consumers, not creators. We like to buy brand-new and expensive things to look rich, even though we're not. Ignorance makes us spend unnecessarily.

Our culture promotes sexy, hot swag and anything flashy, but never true wealth building. Our men want to look trim, wearing the most expensive trainers, trying to outdo one another instead of making money and investing it.

We spend because of cheap and easy access to credit—too much available credit, such as credit cards and bank loans. We forget that it is easy to create debt but difficult to pay it off. Buy now, pay later! Then we all rush to acquire whatever they're selling to make the companies richer but put *you* out of pocket.

Remember: never spend tomorrow's income today. Doing so creates debt, not wealth. You cannot afford to inject poverty into your bloodline, blaming the devil and everyone around you for your family's situation. Do you have an expensive spouse who likes everything they see? It's time you had wise words together.

Overspending on groceries, everyday fast food, and liquor without budgeting will make you poor. Prioritizing beautification and looking glam without planning will lead to impulse and spontaneous purchases, causing you to buy things you will regret one day. And beware of teleshopping!

Some people buy miracle diets and weird fitness products when they could just walk, run, and eat healthy to reduce their expenditure. That goes for pets too—people spend too much on pet food, veterinarians, and even insurance when they cannot afford it.

Our YOLO mentality leads us to take too many outings. We think that since we only live once, it should be parties all the way, with new clothes every time there's a new party to attend.

Are you a loyal customer of Starbucks, Costa, Eat, Cafe Nero, or Pret's? Do you buy takeaway teas and coffees when you could make your own at home to take to work? To save money, or you could take along your favoured drink in powdered form and add hot water when you get to your destination.

Games, the latest technology and in-app purchases, smoking and vaping … all are big money wasters.

Get-rich-quick schemes, also known as a Ponzi or pyramid scheme, are making people waste their money, even sending some to an early grave. Or are you gambling or betting? Remember that wealth is built with consistency, and it takes time, not one day or six months. Investing in good assets requires character, patience, good behaviour, learning, humility, and understanding.

Money doesn't care about your race or religion. It needs respect and handling with care. You can apply the wisdom of seduction to money—think carefully before you give it away. Let that money know that you want to keep it, and it will be yours forever.

Remember that fools are easily parted with their money. And as Proverbs 17:16 reminds, what good is money in the hands of a fool without the desire to seek wisdom?

> There is treasure to be desired and oil in the dwelling of the wise; but a foolish man spends it up. (Proverbs 21:20, Jubilation Bible 2000)

Would you like your generations to have lots of options and freedom in life, and to be secure economically? Would you like to take worry, struggle, and wanting out of your bloodline? By avoiding debt, spending wisely, saving, investing, and building generational wealth, you can—even on a low income.

This book is about eliminating certain behaviours that keeps you poor and adopting behaviours that help you to build wealth across the generations. Wealth building is intentional and requires massive action.

Foreword

Having worked and mentored Mary for a while, I noticed her zeal for advising, helping and supporting others to make better choices in their quest to build generational wealth.

The passion she has for making sure people manage their finances is beyond understanding. Mary, as much as all financial coaches and advisors believe that budgeting, spending less, saving and investing in yourself and your family is the number one requirement for building generational wealth, the reason why I support Mary's vision of Wealth Building.

Emmanuel Asuquo is a Financial Advisor as seen on BBC One, ITV and Channel 4 empowering people to make better financial choices in order to build generational wealth. He is the founder of The Eman Effect and has worked with Halifax Bank, Lloyds, RBS, Barclays, Natwest, HSBC, BBC, Channel 4. Emmanuel specializes in Mortgages, pensions, Life Protections and investments. He has also been featured on ITV, Daily Express, Chanel 4, MW Management, The Sun and Money Marketing. He has been invited as a guest to speak on BBC Radio on multiple occasions. He has worked on projects such as:

Channel 4 in 2019 - Save Well, Spend better
BBC Radio 2021 - Your Money and Your Life
BBC 1 Watchdog - Rip off Britain
ITV Morning Shows
Channel 4 - Secret Spenders

As your net worth consist of your Assets and Liabilites, specifically in Real estates, Investments, Pensions, Life Insurance, Belvedere Wealth Management can help you build wealth and so build generational wealth by securing all of these.

Emmanuel is the Senior Partner of Belvedere Wealth Management located at Canary Wharf in London.

https://belvederewm.com
https://emmanuelasuquo.com

Mary is a passionate professional investment banker well-established in the financial industry. In this book, she uses her industry knowledge and experience to enrich and empower the average citizen in a language that is easy to understand and relatable. This allows a bigger audience to connect with such informative, life-changing information to begin making better financial decisions. Mary helps her readers to master their finances by using engaging financial management examples that encourages them to rethink their mindset about money.

Her book helps you to build a better relationship with money by using everyday and relatable examples.

Mary's book can be set apart from the other financial books because it is knowledgeable, easy to read and to understand, captures and keeps your attention whilst provoking you to want a better financial outcome and to change for the better. Rest assured, Mary will challenge you to reflect on why you are in the situation at hand and offers suggestions to help you get out of it whilst remaining non-judgemental and sympathetic like a good aunt that has your best interests at heart.

Annette Galloway
Financial Educator
CEO Saver to Investor

What Is Generational Wealth?

According to Investopedia.com,[1]

> Wealth measures the value of all the assets of worth owned by a person, community, company, or country. Wealth is determined by taking the total market value of all physical and intangible assets owned, then subtracting all debts. Essentially, wealth is the accumulation of scarce resources. Specific people, organizations, and nations are said to be wealthy when they are able to accumulate many valuable resources or goods. Wealth can be contrasted to income in that wealth is a stock and income is a flow, and it can be seen in either absolute or relative terms.

Generational wealth is wealth that is passed down from one generation to the next through the accumulation of assets that provide financial security for the future. Generational

---

[1] 'Understanding Wealth: How Is It Defined and Measured?' Investopedia (10 July 2022), accessed 12 October 2022, https://www.investopedia.com/terms/w/wealth.asp.

wealth is also called family wealth, multigenerational wealth, or legacy wealth—it's wealth that is passed down from one generation to the next, and it can take many forms, such as heirlooms, traditions, good genes, and a good name. Generally it's thought of as financial wealth, but it is also about preserving your family name. Generational wealth builds a legacy, and building generational wealth takes many lifetimes. If someone should ask you your great-grandfather's name, would you know it? If not, it might be because he did not build any name or legacy to pass on to his generations. To build generational wealth is to build on the financial success of past generations, consciously erasing the poverty mindset and replacing it with the financial education enjoyed by the wealthy elite.

There are four principles of generational wealth:

1. **legacy**, passing on money, knowledge, family missions and values, and traditions
2. **leadership**, the family council as a source of learning, growing, serving, and nurturing
3. **financial wealth**, a foundation of family funds, savings, protection (insurances), and positive money habits.
4. **family lending**, borrowing from the foundation for opportunities and investing in human capital and replenishing it.

Generational wealth is built by acquiring stable assets over generations. The first generation typically works hard to build assets for the second generation to manage, build on, enjoy, and then pass down to their children, who will be the third generation. And so the process goes. Anybody can become rich, but staying rich is the problem. In reality, only a few are able to build generational wealth. These are the people who are hardworking and know the value of money, the people who save, invest, and grow their money instead of spending it, and who have the well-being of their generations at heart.

To succeed at creating generational wealth, you have to teach all the skills you learned to your children. Groom your children for financial success, advise them as necessary, and give them directions along the way. If you don't, be assured that whoever inherits your wealth will blow through it and break the chain of wealth creation.

Build Wealth, Build Your Name

Hilton, Ferrari, Lamborghini, Ford, Chevrolet, Benz, Versace, Louis Vuitton, Ballenciaga, Bosch, Dell, Hewlett-Packard, Harley Davidson, Guinness, Harrods, Marriott, Rolls Royce, Kellogg, McDonalds, Forbes, Fendi, Guicci, the Ritz Carlton … all these companies were started by an individual and built with the family name.

Many businesses survive through time. One person's brain child can become a business that survives for generations, if it is structured in such a way. Everything about the companies above is someone's legacy. The family name becomes the brand and the business—yes, the last name of the family. What would your last name sound like as a brand? Can you start something that your generations can feel involved in and carry the torch forever?

If you build a good brand name, the only requirement

is to keep innovating. Teach your children how to make, grow, and maintain wealth. Make your children part of the company. Mentor your kids to take over your business and build it even bigger than you did. If your children don't start well and do well, then you have failed big time. You are the mentor and the teacher; guide them well, and they will be inspired by your journey.

Marry well, because if you have to divorce at a certain point, you or your children could say goodbye to the wealth that took you years to build.

To build generational wealth, you need to distinguish between personal and family wealth. Personal wealth is for one person and mostly comes in the form of cash assets, which are liquid or can be liquidated quickly, such as money in a bank account or stocks and shares of products. Family wealth is more illiquid and cannot be easily converted to cash, or further steps would be needed to change it to cash. Because of the nature of family wealth, the assets tend to be preserved for generations and are less likely to be blown through.

Build businesses, and expand them as time goes on. Building businesses will make you money now, and even when you are dead and gone, your name will continue to make money. Don't just do jobs that make you miserable—fulfil your purpose.

Here are some practical ways to build wealth.

Stocks. If you want your investment money to grow, buy stocks and shares through indexes such as the S&P 500, FTSE 100, and FTSE 250. Over time and with the help of compound interest, your money will grow exponentially. Statistically, the FTSE and S&P consistently have annual increases of 6–10 percent. You can invest through financial services companies such as Hargreaves Lansdown, Vanguard, or Fidelity. With these types of investments, you buy and hold for a longer term. Even if you need money short-term, do not withdraw or sell your holdings. Just leave them to compound and accumulate. Never sell an asset—I repeat, never sell an investment asset. Find money on the side to cover whatever you need.

Property. Buy land so you can keep it forever. Population is increasing, and demand for space is shooting up. Cash-flow properties include apartments and commercial properties, which you buy, hold, and wait as prices increase. Rental income is passive income that will always feed your family.

Precious metals and art. You can also buy and hold precious metals as a way of building generational wealth. If necessary, these assets can be pawned rather than borrowed against. Buy and hold artwork. There is value in collectibles, and the value of art has stood the test of time.

Taxes and interest. Never stop earning, but minimise your taxes. Be 100 percent legal, but find ways to reduce your tax. Tap into the power of compound interest; it is the main key to wealth building. Compound wealth *and* knowledge—the more you know, the better decisions you will make.

Trusts and wills. You can set up trusts to protect your wealth. A trust is a legal arrangement that protects, manages, and distributes wealth according to your instructions. Write your will. Everybody will die one day, and your wishes need to be protected. A will makes sure your wealth ends up in good hands.

That's how you build wealth—and generational wealth.

Why Build Generational Wealth?

Inherited wealth may be something easily squandered, but inherited poverty is a legacy almost impossible to lose.
Eric L. Haney

A good man leaves an inheritance to his children's children.
Proverbs 13:22

Nobody wants to live with poverty or to see their family struggling to make ends meet. Sadly, a lot of families do live with poverty from one generation to the next, so people should want to build assets that last to see their generations through life's challenges. People who are indebted often go through periods of stress, sickness, and disease, and these issues can even be passed down to future generations. So instead of generational blessings, that family will have generational curses—all because of poverty.

Obviously, people who inherit wealth from previous generations have advantages over others. For example, students who don't need to borrow money for tuition fees and student accommodations will not start life overwhelmed with debt. With generational wealth comes the ability to avoid student loans as well as other debts that could cost young people their livelihoods. Instead of debts, they are able to invest their inheritance into other income-generating assets, which will constantly appreciate in value to pay for their lifestyle and even their first home.

The challenge here is maintaining these assets over time and across generations. Seventy percent of families lose their wealth in the second generation. Building wealth requires more than knowledge. It entails hard work, discipline, sacrifice, and other traits that are hard to teach and pass on. Typically, the first generation is the generation that experiences hardship in working and building wealth to achieve something better. This generation works hard to build assets, to live a better life in retirement, and to leave some for their following generations. The next generation will also see what their parents struggled with whilst building wealth and will have good understanding as to how wealth is built. They will understand the value of sacrifice and hard work. Since they are aware of what their parents went through, some will make better financial, educational, and life decisions growing up. The third generation will grow up with their needs met by the wealth they were born into and will lack understanding of what is needed to create and maintain the lifestyle they have grown accustomed to. So it is estimated that 90 percent of wealthy families will lose their wealth by the third generation.[2]

David Kleinhandler notes a few of the reasons that wealth is lost over the generations.

- Generations are taught not to talk about money
- The prior generations worry that the next generation will become lazy and entitled
- Many have no clue about the value of money or how to handle it

Most parents find it very difficult to discuss their wealth, and what happens when they're gone with their children. Whatever the reasons for lack of transparency, the failure to discuss will likely

---

[2] David Kleinhandler, 'Generational Wealth: Why do 70% of Families Lose Their Wealth in the 2nd Generation?' Nasdaq Smart Investing series (19 October 2018), https://www.nasdaq.com/articles/generational-wealth%3A-why-do-70-of-families-lose-their-wealth-in-the-2nd-generation-2018-10.

end with such issues like unnecessary taxes, costly estate fees, and possible family strife. Also, by not detailing their intentions, you run the risk of eroding the value of your estate.

The families that do maintain their multi-generational wealth are able to do so by communicating with the next generations in a very straightforward manner. The rules they live by to do this are very simple but not always easy. These tips can be used by anyone who wants to have a successful conversation about wealth with their children.

1. **Having Lines of Communication:** Open communication builds the trust that is the basis for sustaining your family's wealth. Preparing the next generation for what they can expect is critical and you should take advantage of any teachable moments that arise. By doing this, the next generation can learn, understand and eventually participate in decisions that can affect the family's wealth. It could also be a good idea to introduce a wealth expert or advisor to help facilitate a productive discussion. This could lead to a better understanding among the family members and help them discover shared values and passions. These values and passions could result in the members to work together and share in decision-making regarding the family wealth. They are also critical in helping them stay together during times of adversity.

2. **Share Decision Making:** More often than not, beneficiaries of family wealth are unable to properly manage what they've inherited. Often this is the result of decisions made by the earlier generations regarding the members' involvement with decisions made managing the wealth. By keeping the next generation out of the decision-making process can lead to serious dysfunction and lead to a serious lack of understanding about how the wealth is managed. They will be lacking the skills needed to ensure they lead a happy and productive life. Without the necessary core values or understanding of their family's goals, the ability to maintain and grow the wealth is lacking.

3. **Consider an Impartial Trustee:** Even with a solid line of communication open and a proper decision-making process

in place, there will still be some challenges that a family will not be able to handle on their own. Having an objective third-party point of view could be useful, freeing any discussions from emotions that family members may bring to the table. Having a Trustee can ensure that your wealth is properly managed and will be distributed properly. If there are intangible assets involved, a trustee, as a neutral party, can protect the beneficiaries over a longer period of time. They can also mediate over emotional attachments that some family members may have over certain items, items that could eventually lead to litigation amongst the family.

4. **Make a Plan:** Here is where you develop a clear goal that plan the direction of the wealth so it is sustained for future generations. Lacking a proper plan could result in the wealth being lost for future generations to taxes, poor investments and unprepared recipients of the wealth. His plan should be a roadmap providing insight on how the wealth should be managed and invested for future generations. Bringing in a Financial Planning Professional, one who has the experience dealing with the areas you want to focus on and handling your level of wealth, should be considered here as well. This can help ensure that there will be something for future generations.

It is nearly impossible to pass on family wealth to the generations beyond your grandchildren and there are plenty of statistics that back that up. There are many pitfalls that you can avoid to make sure that your hard work will last well beyond the third generation. Along with investing wisely and developing a good estate plan, educating the next generations is a crucial element in making your wealth last. Put the values you believe in into practice to sustain your family as well as your fortune.

From David Kleinhandler, "Generational Wealth: Why do 70% of Families Lose Their Wealth in the 2nd Generation?" Nasdaq Smart Investing series (19 October 2018), https://www.nasdaq.com/articles/generational-wealth%3A-why-do-70-of-families-lose-their-wealth-in-the-2nd-generation-2018-10.

How to Teach Your Kids to Be Investors

In order to teach your kids about generational wealth, you have to learn and master it yourself. Be disciplined with money, avoid bad debt, and build wealth by investing in land, buildings, businesses, stocks and shares, mutual funds, gold, collectibles, trust funds, bonds, and other assets.

Children learn by watching what adults do, so if you're not investing yourself, how do you expect your children to learn from you? You need to learn how to invest properly and teach your children along the way. You need to pass down more than money to your heirs, or they will not know how to preserve and grow inherited wealth. Teach them the value of money and of making money and keeping some for themselves first. Teach your children the rule of hard work by understanding the business. Make sure the business has a competitive advantage over others, work with people you trust, and buy into the margin of safety.

Generational wealth cannot be built in a single generation, with the exception of a very few families. You may not have much money in the first generation, but you can start by transferring wealth to the next generation, who will manage and build upon it. Real generational wealth continues from the first generation, through the second, and into the third generation and beyond. The only way to ensure a long line of inheritors is for generational wealth to be a gown worn by everyone in the family.

2

How to Build Generational Wealth

To build generational wealth, you have to offer value for money. You have to render services or produce something of value in order to get money and lay down strategies to manage your wealth. It is not the absence of money that makes a person poor but the management of money you do receive if you do not give value to it. Honesty, integrity, and the ability to keep promises are forms of intangible wealth which can also be exchanged for or converted to cash. Where there is integrity, there is trust.

To build generational wealth:

- **Produce something.** Produce goods and services. Research and find out what goods are in high demand, and produce them in large quantities, depending on demand. You can grow agricultural products, manufacture products, or offer services.
- **Own something.** Own houses, bonds, mutual funds, stocks and shares, businesses, or other assets.
- **Invest.** Invest like a professional. Investments compound and accumulate over the years, so leave investments intact to gain the benefit of compound interest.

- **Save.** Save money with a bank for easy access in case you need it whilst gaining interest paid on these savings.
- **Be an entrepreneur.** Entrepreneurs are people who set up their own business, taking on all the risks in the hope of making profit. To be a successful entrepreneur, you have to have passion and be self-motivated, understand what you want to offer, and be able to take risk. You must be a networker and understand that no man is an Island. You must have knowledge and skills in money management, or you will lose a lot of money. To start a new business, know what your passion is and develop it further. Keep in mind that Coca-Cola, KFC, Pizza Hut, Hilton Hotels, Ebay, and Alibaba all started small but now are huge. You can start a hotel from a modest Airbnb and build it up.

To build generational wealth, you will need to adhere to certain principles. Work to earn income which will be spent on your needs but also can be saved and invested. Learning money management will propel you toward building wealth.

A Pillar of Wealth: Compound Interest

Someone is sitting in the shade today because someone planted a tree long time ago.
Warren Buffett

Merely saving your money in a normal savings account will earn you simple interest. A major difference between wealthy people and poor people is stock market participation, which offers compound interest. Compound interest means getting interest on top of the interest you've already earned when you save or invest. Compound interest works in reverse for debt: instead of getting more money, you are paying more money on top of what you owe someone, whether your bank or an individual. Compound interest works better with stocks and shares-related investments rather than cash. You accumulate more with stocks and shares. In recent decades, ordinary savings accounts have paid very low or almost no interest. Stocks overall are riskier, or at least individual stocks may be, but a mutual fund over time brings in a much greater rate of return than a savings account at a bank.

Your aim should be to transform yourself from being a labourer who sells his time for money into a capitalist who uses the same money to earn more money. In other words, let your money work for you whilst you sleep. To build wealth, long-term thinking is required so that your money accumulates and grows through the power of compound interest.

As you build wealth, incorporate financial education into your family. Get everybody on board so they can understand how to earn money and how to keep it. A lack of financial education will do more harm to children than the good of inheriting millions without the knowledge to manage money.

Making Use of Compound Interest

Below are examples of investment calculations. Figure 2.1 shows a consistent monthly investment of £200 with earnings at 12% compound interest over a period of ten years, with end results of up to £47,000. The same monthly investment of £200 for twenty years will earn you around

£200,000 (Fig. 2.2); for thirty years, around £700,000 (Fig. 2.3); and forty years, around £2,400,000 (Fig. 2.4).

FIGURE 2.1. Investing £200 for ten years at a return rate of 12%

INPUTS		
Principal		£200.00
Interest		12 %
Compound		Monthly
Duration	10	Years
Additions ±	£200.00	Monthly
	at start of period	

RESULTS	
Total Interest	£22,927.89
Total Additions	£24,000.00
Ending Balance	£47,127.89

FIGURE 2.2. Investing £200 for twenty years at a return rate of 12%

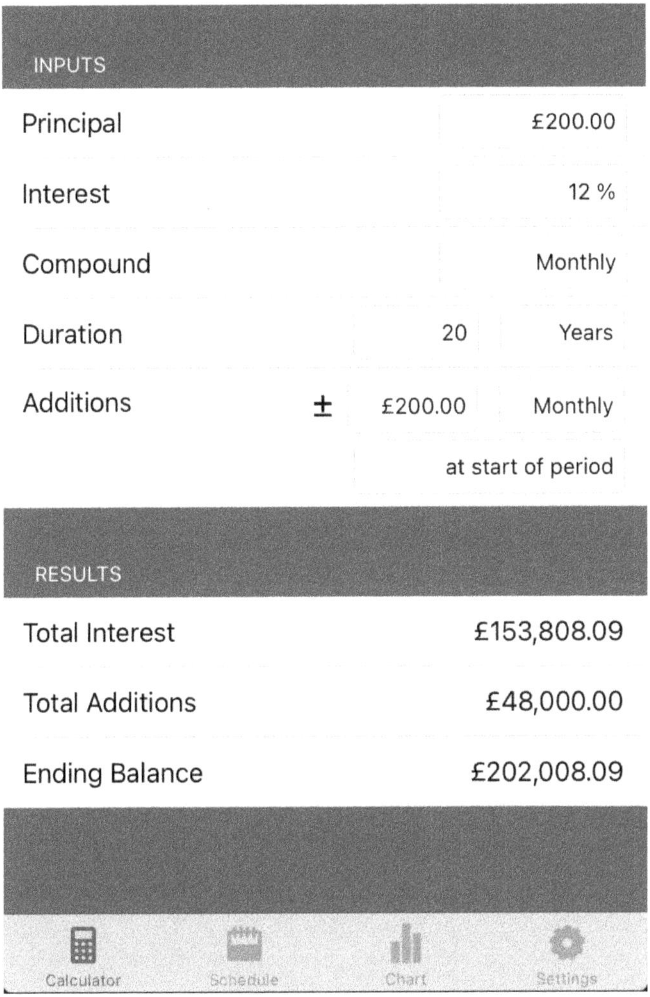
INPUTS
Principal
£200.00
Interest
12 %
Compound
Monthly
Duration
20
Years
Additions
±
£200.00
Monthly
at start of period
RESULTS
Total Interest
£153,808.09
Total Additions
£48,000.00
Ending Balance
£202,008.09
Calculator
Schedule
Chart
Settings

FIGURE 2.3. Investing £200 for thirty years at a return rate of 12%

INPUTS

Principal	£200.00
Interest	12 %
Compound	Monthly
Duration	30 Years
Additions ±	£200.00 Monthly
	at start of period

RESULTS

Total Interest	£640,972.68
Total Additions	£72,000.00
Ending Balance	£713,172.68

Calculator · Schedule · Chart · Settings

FIGURE 2.4. Investing £200 for forty years at a return rate of 12%

INPUTS		
Principal		£200.00
Interest		12 %
Compound		Monthly
Duration	40	Years
Additions ±	£200.00	Monthly
		at start of period

RESULTS	
Total Interest	£2,304,013.59
Total Additions	£96,000.00
Ending Balance	£2,400,213.59

However, when you increase your monthly investment to £500 for forty years, you will earn around £6,000,000

(Fig. 2.5). The longer the term of investment, the greater your chances of accumulating more.

FIGURE 2.5. Investing £500 for forty years at a return rate of 12%

INPUTS	
Principal	£500.00
Interest	12 %
Compound	Monthly
Duration	40 Years
Additions	± £500.00 Monthly
	at start of period

RESULTS	
Total Interest	£5,760,033.98
Total Additions	£240,000.00
Ending Balance	£6,000,533.98

You might question the interest rate applied to the investment. However, if you do your research well, you will find a good growth fund earning such a rate over time. When your children are still quite young, invest for them in an aggressive growth mutual fund, such as Exchange Traded Funds (ETFs), index funds, and individual stocks. Providing a solid foundation for building generational wealth requires a shift in your thinking. Become a long-time investor and not a waster. Think and plan for the long term instead of for weeks or months.

Merely saving your money in a normal savings account attracts only simple interest and little growth. If you don't know how much and where to invest, self-education is key. You can conduct your own research on the Hargreaves Lansdown platform, Vanguard, AJ Bell, Barclays Smart Investor, Schwab, E-Trade, M1 Finance, or Fidelity, where you can choose a fund or single stock to invest in. With these in mind, you fire and forget—meaning, you can invest, forget that you have some monies sitting somewhere, and let the investment accumulate further into the future.

Improving Your Finances Is a Necessity

*Rich people plan for three generations,
poor people plan for Saturday night.*
Gloria Steinem

People who do not manage their finances well will always feel their hearts racing when they open a bill. Some will even ignore bills, piling up debt, further damaging their credit score, and affecting their ability to obtain credit for a mortgage, car loan, or credit card. They always feel like their world is falling apart because they have hardly any money for unexpected expenses and no emergency funds.

When you improve your finances, you will be able to afford nice things and live a comfortable life. It gives you the chance to quit a job you hate to start your own business, inspire others, and take control of your own life. You will understand the need to be free of debt and can be debt-free forever, giving your children and your grandchildren more opportunities in life and becoming a blessing to them and not a curse. You will be able to retire early with dignity without recourse to the public purse or dependency on family and friends. Improving your own finances will mean ensuring your children and grandchildren never live in poverty. You can change the course of your family tree and bloodline, in the process becoming more charitable—just think of the opportunities to contribute to good causes you are passionate about.

Wealth building is all about time and money. You need time to accumulate wealth, and the amount of monies invested will determine how big your investment pot will be. Ordinary people spend over 60% of their income on needs, over 35% on wants, and a mere 5% or less on savings and investments—or sometimes nothing at all. As they earn more income, they tend to increase their liabilities, so they end up back at square one. Or as Parkinson's law states, no matter how your income increases, expenses will always rise to meet income. By contrast, finance-conscious people will spend 40% on needs and 10% on wants while investing the remaining 50% to build more wealth.

In this chapter, we will look at some steps to get you started on your path to building wealth.

Budgeting

A budget is an estimate of future income and expenditure. A budget helps you live within your means. It encourages you to watch what comes into your accounts in the form of income, and what goes out of your account as expenses.

To budget effectively, you need to have a "why"—why do you want to budget? Do you want to spend less to save more of your money so you can invest for your future? Or do you want to invest for your children's education? To raise a deposit to buy a house? To buy a car?

To budget is to analyse, brainstorm, and then change something., You can use a challenge tracker to encourage yourself to budget. Analyse what is happening now as in your income and expenditure, then brainstorm on what can be changed for the future. What can you do? What are some ideas you can use to change something? You have to commit to changing something specific, but they should be big things. Make physical changes. Change big expenses to make a big difference.

For example, stop going to the mall, because it will attract you to spend. Just do your grocery shopping. If you have a big house in a nice neighbourhood, consider moving to a smaller house. If you have two cars, consider selling the second car to unlock capital and save on fuel, insurance, and servicing.

You can track your expenditure weekly or monthly. If you live pay check to pay check, always plan for the long term, and delay instant gratification. Allocate your finances with an eye on financial independence, and know where your money come from. Know your sources of income by using a spreadsheet. Determine how much money comes in weekly or monthly. You can do this by going through your bank statements and credit card statements.

When your income is more than your expenditure, you have a positive cash flow. But if your expenditure exceeds your income, you have a negative cash flow, so find ways to cut, reduce, or maintain your expenditures.

If you have a credit card with a higher interest rate, try calling the financial institution to renegotiate. Too many credit accounts? Consider refinancing and consolidating old debt at a lower interest rate so you can pay off credit cards more quickly, freeing money for saving or investments.

Assign a certain percentage of your income to your expenditures and distribute the rest among short-term savings, long-term investments, your financial freedom account, education, fun, and giving. When you do this, you will clearly see where all your money is allocated. Cracking the code between income and expenditure is all you need to build wealth. Wealth creation comes not just from income but the way you spend it and the difference left after all expenditures. This is why you have to manage your expenditures well. Merely paying out your money without budgeting is a sure way to lose wealth.

Assets

An individual's net worth is the value of all assets minus all liabilities owed. It's an important metric to ascertain a person's financial standing. When positive, it means you are doing well or have a healthy financial position. A negative net worth means your liabilities exceed your assets. High-net-worth individuals are those whose liquid assets or investible wealth exceeds a certain figure, usually set at around a million.

The best way to improve a negative net worth is to reduce your liabilities and increase your assets. *Own* more, and reduce your *owing*.

Assets are the things you own such as land, buildings, cash in the bank, investment account balances, stocks or bonds, and automobiles, whilst liabilities are what you owe to individuals or banks, such as mortgages, car loans, and credit cards.

Assets can be static, such as properties, or income-producing, such as stocks, bonds, rental properties and royalty incomes. Most millionaires have seven streams of income such as earned Income from your salary at work, income from your businesses, income from your bank account savings, dividend income from stocks and shares, income from rental properties, capital gains on various assets, royalty income from books or other recurring income you have set up. To build wealth, you need more income-producing assets than static assets so you can take advantage of compound interest. Choose investment vehicles that are tax-favoured like an ISA, 401(k), or IRA, as any income from these are free from taxation.

Increasing Income and Reducing Expenditures

The habit of savings itself is an education: it fosters every virtue: teaches self denial, cultivates the sense of order, trains to forethought and so broadens the mind.
T. T. Munger

If after all your expenses are made you have nothing left, then consider yourself living in poverty. But if for example you have £100 left, invest this amount consistently so that over the long term you can build wealth. If you can find a way to increase this £100 to say £500, and invest this £500 monthly, then you are sure to become wealthy. The difference between income and expenditure is expressed by a delta (Δ). Find ways of increasing your delta through reduction of expenditures or an increase of income.

If you are an employee, work hard to impress your boss and ask for a raise, work more hours, or even better, find a higher paying job than the one you have. Take on a second job or create a side business. Rent out a spare room if you have one.

To reduce expenditures, downsize your home or trade down your car—if your car is too flashy and expensive, and it's a pure liability that isn't bringing in any income, sell it and buy a more affordable one. Shop for groceries from budget shops such as Aldi, Lidl, or Asda. If you are a smoker, stop smoking. Pets are very expensive, so if you don't have one already, consider how monthly pet maintenance would dent your pockets. Pay for your insurance policies ahead so you do not pay interest on them.

When you reduce your outgoings, you are able to keep more of your income to maximise your savings and investments

Avoid the Scarcity Mindset

Financial experts advise keeping an emergency fund, avoiding debt, and saving and investing even if you earn little income. When you put monies away by investing, it accumulates and continues to accumulate over time, giving you a sense of purpose, achievement, confidence, and stability. Without investing, you will develop a scarcity mindset which is a dangerous mindset to keep and a barrier to your success. Mehrsa Baradaran explains this mindset in *The Color of Money*:

> A state of scarcity is such a heavy mental burden that it can lead to temporarily lower cognitive ability and shortsighted decision making. This does not mean that the poor have less capacity but that their capacity is over burdened because living in scarcity takes up significant mental space and leaves less room for other mental processes. Those operating under the pressure of scarcity have been shown to eat poorly, parent poorly, make bad decisions and even wash their hands less often. Scarcity also creates tunnelling which is a hyper-focused mindset that homes in on the resource in scarcity.[3]

This is the kind of mindset I pray none of your descendants develop. It is a waste of time in the midst of abundance to develop such a negative mindset, as it keeps you stuck.

As you build wealth, your mindset changes, and your thoughts becomes actions. I will say it again: to arrive at financial freedom, find a way to reduce your outgoings, do not create further debt, save, invest, and think of the longer term. Set goals of ten, twenty, thirty, and even forty years. Read more and acquire new skills that will help you earn money to build wealth.

With the scarcity mindset, you make terrible mistakes and bad decisions. You are likely to take on credit card debt or a loan to supplement income and pay for small purchases,

---

[3] Mehrsa Baradaran, *The Color of Money: Black Banks and the Racial Wealth Gap* (Cambridge, MA: Belknap Press, 2017), p. 252.

hence building more debt and putting your health at risk. Change this negative mindset to change your family tree.

To build generational wealth, there is a starting point of one person, and that can be you. Every change can start within you first. Wealth is built internally, not externally. Externalities are those things you do not have control over, such as who your prime minister or president is. You cast only one vote, and the rest is done by others, so the onus does not fall entirely on you in choosing a president. You do not choose your boss, the employment rate, stock market performance, and the rate of inflation—these are all externalities you do not have control over. But the way your money is spent relies solely on your management. If you understand that you are in control of your destiny, you can focus all your energy and attention on making it a better one.

Having control of your own money is the first major step to helping your children build generational wealth. Define what you want to achieve in life and your intended actions to make this plan succeed, and constantly measure the outcome against your plan. For example, your plan might include the following goals:

- avoid impulse purchases
- not borrow any money and manage what you already make
- save a certain amount of money or percentage of your income
- invest in high-growth and stable stocks
- buy your first home within a particular time frame (say, in two, three, or five years) or even invest in rental properties

Make your goals clear, specific, measurable, realistic, and achievable within a timeline.

The best generational wealth you can give your descendants is not be a burden on them in old age, which would not be fair as you had the opportunity to change the narrative. You cannot waste money today and expect your future generations to bear the cost of your carelessness. Change your mindset today.

4

Home Ownership and Investment Property

For many people, home equity is by far their biggest chunk of wealth. Everybody needs a roof over their heads, but merely renting a home is like paying someone else's mortgage for them, making them richer and you poorer. Over the years, real estate creates equity, which forms part of your net worth. So buying your own home is key, a major life step, and everybody's dream. But before you buy a home as a first-time buyer, make sure you have a steady income for at least three years and no current debt payments or default, doing this will help you get a mortgage with a better interest rate. Also make sure you have some emergency funds as a back-up for extra expenditure and your deposit monies.

There are many incentives for buying your first home, depending on the country you live in.

Help to Buy

In the UK, we have the Help to Buy equity loan, where the government of the United Kingdom will support first-time buyers with up to 20% of the deposit, to which the buyer adds 5% to make the total 25% deposit—meaning that the buyer then finances 75% of home's cost as a mortgage, however there are restrictions and the buyer may need to qualify. The government's loan is interest-free for the first five years, after which monthly interest will be applied. This is a great help for people unable to come up with the total deposit needed to purchase their first home. This deal might be changing so always do your research for alternatives.

Right to Buy

The Right to Buy scheme is an excellent opportunity to own a home by buying your council house or housing association home at a discount, giving you instant equity.

First Homes

The First Homes scheme, launched in June 2021, gives first-time buyers the opportunity to buy their home at a 30% discount. First Homes is available only to first-time buyers in England buying a new property. Purchasers must have a household income of less than £80,000 (or £90,000 in London).The scheme is designed to help people get on the housing ladder in their local area. Eligibility criteria are set by the local authority and may differ from place to place. For example, priority may be given to local key workers. There are only a handful of developments that offer First Homes, but more sites are due to launch across the country, with a further 1,500 homes for sale.

Mortgage Guarantee

With a mortgage guarantee, the government guarantees 95% of the property value whilst the buyer only secures this property with a 5% deposit. With this type of mortgage, first time buyers and existing homeowners can apply and as with all mortgage application, you must be employed with regular income and a good credit rating. In the event of a default, the promise from the government is to underwrite 15% of the mortgage for both new build and old properties that cost less than £600,000.[4]

Shared Ownership

Shared ownership gives you an opportunity to buy a share of the property, for example 25%, 30%, or 50%. You pay rent on the share you do not own. Shared ownership gives you an opportunity to get on the property ladder. You buy a small percentage, and as your financial position improves, you increase your percentage until you finally own 100% of the property. This is called staircasing.

Lifetime ISA

A Lifetime ISA (LISA) is a type of account designed to encourage people to save for their first home or their retirement. You can save up to £4,000 a year, and the government will top this up with a 25% bonus.

Rent to Buy

Another UK Government scheme is the Rent to Buy which gives you the opportunity to rent a brand-new home with the intention to buy later.

---

[4] 'Government Home Buying Schemes in 2022', HomeOwners Alliance, accessed 14 October 2022, https://hoa.org.uk/advice/guides-for-homeowners/i-am-buying/government-schemes-help-buy-home.

Investment Properties

An asset is an investment that brings you income. Property investment is one of the best ways to build wealth, with future income streams through rental yields. Real estate is a brick-and-mortar, tangible asset. A rental property is an asset because it brings in passive income, and property appreciates in value. Investment properties can give you monthly income through rentals and additional wealth through capital appreciation (equity or capital gains).

Before investing, watch market trends for movements in the property market. Is the market going up, down, or sideways? Is there currently any negative growth or potential for positive growth (e.g. planned development or regeneration) in the future? Potential regeneration in that area will gradually push prices up.

It is advisable to have the investment property close to your house to avoid extra monitoring or management costs. Fall in love with the area first before the house. Area first, property second. You can always improve the looks of the house but not the area. View as many properties as you can. Know your budget before you go in. Try viewing the properties both day and night. On the day of your viewing, take a damp-proof meter with you, or better yet do a full survey of the property. Do not be afraid to move furniture around so you can investigate properly. Are they hiding anything behind these furnishings? Check whether the doors and windows close properly. Is the roofing in a good state? Replacement roofing costs a lot, so do your checks properly or you will be handed a huge bill later.

Sometime you can buy off-plan properties at a slightly

lower amount, and by the time the home is completely built, the price will appreciate and you either sell to take your profit or keep to rent out. You can also find property deals and negotiate a discount. Find ways to finance the property deal and manage it by renting.

Why Properties?

Property is a more stable asset compared to stocks and shares, and you have 100% control—there is no principal and agent relationship as with stockbrokers. Not everyone is able to buy their own home, so there is always demand for rental properties, which give you a constant stream of income.

Properties always appreciate in value and it is my observation that every ten years property prices double, so even a bear market always ends up as a bull market. When value goes down, just give it time to readjust—no need to sell.

There are two types of property investment: HMOs and property flips.

An HMO (house in multiple occupation) is a property having three or more tenants, with toilets, kitchen, and common room all shared. HMOs have attractive rental yield not common with ordinary buy-to-let. When a tenant moves out, a tenant is still in occupation, so you never lose out. Before investing in HMOs, research first. Read up on HMOs, and speak with your local HMO officer who helps landlords.

Property flips are bought and sold in twelve months. To invest in a flip, always research first. Buy at a discount and not the full price, as you need to factor in closing cost, commission, insurances, taxes, and mortgages. It's best to use cash for renovation so your cost will reduce and maybe the market value remain competitive. Buy from owners, bank auctions, or a housing wholesaler so you can negotiate price—because once listed, it gets pricey. The house should be right without too much work. Focus on the kitchen, bathroom, systems, and appliances, and make sure you have the education, time, and financial support team all in place to take off.

Financing Investment Properties

It is possible to buy an investment property even if you don't have enough cash. Loans from banks are the most popular form of financing a property investment, but it can be very difficult and complicated process. Banks require that you have a certain percentage of the required funds available, which you may not have. But do not be discouraged, as there are creative financing techniques such as borrowing from private lenders. The criteria used by private lenders, whether corporate or personal private lenders, are not as rigid as those of banks, making it quicker to decide on a case.

Personal private lenders can be your friend, relative, or even close family member. Using other people's money (OPM) can be cheaper than borrowing from the banks. You might be able to partner up with a friend or relative, with or someone you don't even know, to complete specific projects.

Another way of funding a property investment project is to tap into your home equity. Explore the options available to you, and don't be limited by lack of funds—remember, you're building generational wealth.

5

Stocks and Mutual Funds

*The stock market is a device for transferring money
from the impatient to the patient.*
Warren Buffett

A stock is a share of ownership in a publicly traded company, allowing people to build wealth through ownership in companies. When a company needs money for a project, the company first markets itself to big investors. If they think it's a good idea and worth it, they get the first opportunity to invest by raising an initial public offering (IPO). After this is done, then the holders of the shares can buy more or sell through the open stock market, and other people can also buy and sell.

The IPO launches the company onto the official stock market where any company or individual can buy and sell stocks. Buying stocks will make the investors partial owners in the business. Their investment will help the company to grow. Growth is reflected in the share price and will attract more investors to the company. When the company makes more profits, they will declare dividends and pay out to their shareholders.

However, it is risky to own single stocks, as any negative effect on the company will affect its share price and dividends, so investor gurus advise that one of the best forms of long-term investment is buying stocks, shares, and bonds through mutual funds. A mutual fund allows you to buy small portions of several different stocks. However, before you invest in a mutual fund, check for fees, as some charge higher fees than others. Managed funds come with higher fees, whilst others such as index funds come with lower fees.

An index fund is a type of mutual fund or exchange traded fund (ETF) which invests in a representative range of all stocks on the stock market; for example, the iShares Core FTSE 100 UCITS ETF, which tracks the whole of the FTSE 100, or the Vanguard 500, which tracks the S&P. An index fund is designed with a portfolio to track or mimic the performance of a specific financial market. It allows your money to be part of a larger pool of money to buy assets on the stock market, matching the returns and risks associated with the stock market.

The benefits of index funds include better returns, lower fees, and transparency. An index fund gives you the chance to diversify your portfolio, therefore minimising risk. Even though it may lack flexibility, as it tracks and sticks to specifics, an index fund should outperform managed funds. So the best way of growing your money is to invest in index funds, which take advantage of compound interest, instead of in a normal savings account, which only gives you simple interest.

It is sometimes said that cash savers are losers, as your money will lose its purchasing power over time as inflation will cause your money to lose its purchasing power over time.

Most people do not like investing in the stock market because they are afraid of losing their money. Little do they know that even their pension funds are invested in stocks. So the earlier you get rid of the fear and educate yourself on stock-market related products, the better. You can do this through financial services companies such as Hargreaves Lansdown, Vanguard, Fidelity, M1 Finance, AJ Bell, E-Trade, Schwab, Barclays Smart Investor, and so on.

Self-education is important if you want to take your financial destiny into your own hands.

What Are Mutual Funds?

Investor.gov, an informational website by the US Securities and Exchange Commission, gives the following definition:

> A mutual fund is a company that pools money from many investors and invests the money in securities such as stocks, bonds, and short-term debt. The combined

holdings of the mutual fund are known as its portfolio. Investors buy shares in mutual funds. Each share represents an investor's part ownership in the fund and the income it generates.[5]

Mutual funds are very popular with investors because there is a fund manager who performs market research, selects securities, and monitors the funds' performance on your behalf. So you don't need to be an expert in investment to invest in mutual funds.

You may have heard the adage, 'Don't put your eggs in one basket.' Mutual funds invest in a broad range of companies and industries. If one company is not performing well, others will be. This is called diversification of funds.

Mutual funds are set up in a way that anyone can afford, because a lower minimum amount is required for initial and subsequent investments. Mutual funds are also highly liquid; that is, investors are allowed to redeem their shares at any time they wish, based on current net asset value and less any redemption fee.

Types of Mutual Funds

Mutual funds fall into four categories:

1. money market funds
2. bond funds

---

[5] 'Mutual Funds', Investor.gov, accessed 14 October 2022, https://www.investor.gov/investing-basics/investment-products/mutual-funds.

3. stock funds
4. target date funds

Each type of mutual fund has different features, different risks, and different rewards. By far, a money market fund has the lower risks, because by law such a fund can invest only in a certain type of high-quality, short-term investment issued by the local government. Bond funds give higher returns but are a bit riskier than money market funds. Because there are many different types of bonds, the risks and rewards of bond funds can vary dramatically, increasing the level of uncertainty.

There are different kinds of stock funds which invest in corporate stocks, including:

- **growth funds**, comprising stocks with a potential for above-average financial gains that may not pay a regular dividend
- **income funds**, which buy stocks that pay regular dividends
- **index funds**, which as noted above track a particular market index, such as the S&P 500
- **sector funds**, which specialise in buying stocks within a particular industry or market sector[6]

Target date funds holds a mixture of assets, including but not limited to bonds and stocks. After a while, the mix gradually shifts according to the fund's strategy. This type of fund is ideal for investors or individual with a set retirement date in mind.

---

[6] 'Mutual Funds', Investor.gov.

Advantages and Disadvantages of Mutual Funds

As a managed fund with professional investment managers who diversifies portfolio to manage risk, a mutual fund offers many advantages. Investors earn income through dividend payments from stocks or interest payments from bonds after all expenses have been deducted, and dividends can be reinvested.

Securities can also gain value over time, and when the fund sells a security that has increased in value, the fund is said to yield capital gains. These positive returns are redistributed to investors at the end of the year, minus any expenses.

The net asset value (NAV) of an investment can also increase in value if after all expenditure is deducted, the value of the fund and the share price have increased. A higher NAV reflects the higher value of your investment.

Mutual funds also have disadvantages, as the value of the securities can also go down. You may lose some of the money you invested, or sometimes all of it. As market conditions change, dividends and interest payments may be affected.

Investor.com cautions:

> A fund's past performance is not as important as you might think because past performance does not predict future returns. But past performance can tell you how volatile or stable a fund has been over a

period of time. The more volatile the fund, the higher the investment risk.[7]

Mutual Fund Fees

There are fees, costs, and taxes for running or managing mutual funds. These costs are passed down to investors in fees and expenses which vary from fund to fund. A small difference in fees can mean a large difference in returns over time. Here's an example from Investor.com:

> If you invested $10,000 in a fund with a 10% annual return, and annual operating expenses of 1.5%, after 20 years you would have roughly $49,725. If you invested in a fund with the same performance and expenses of 0.5%, after 20 years you would end up with $60,858.[8]

You can use a mutual fund cost calculator to calculate the overall cost of different mutual funds over time to see the real costs that will eat into your returns.

Buying and Selling Mutual Funds

You can buy shares in mutual funds directly with the funds itself or through a broker for the fund instead of from other investors. The price that investors pay for the mutual fund is

---

[7] 'Mutual Funds,' Investor.gov.
[8] 'Mutual Funds', Investor.gov.

the fund's per share net asset value plus any fees charged at the time of purchase, such as sales loads. Shares in mutual funds are redeemable meaning investors can sell shares back to the fund at any time and the fund will pay up within seven days. However, it is always advisable to read the prospectus carefully before buying shares in a mutual fund as the prospectus contains information about the mutual fund's objectives, risks, expenses and performance.

Learning How to Invest

In a nutshell, you can learn a lot about how to invest by following Warren Buffet's annual letters, and reading books such as Mohnish Pabrai's *The Dhandho Investor* and Guy Spier's *The Education of a Value Investor*.

To invest in a business, first understand the nature of the business and management to see whether you share the same values with them. Always buy on a special offer or discount or sale. The best investments are in properties, stocks and shares, Individual Savings Account (ISA), mutual funds, and bonds. But it is also important to know that investment is not only about money—it's also an investment in people. So get out there and meet new people, network, and remember that we are to love one another. Find something you're passionate about and focus on serving others' needs. People are created to be givers and takers, but there is more blessing in giving than receiving.

Other Aspects of Personal Finance

In this chapter, we'll look at three other important tools for managing your personal finances toward creating generational wealth: pensions, life insurance, and writing a will.

Pensions

A pension is money put away until you reach a certain age or are no longer able to work. The earliest age you can take a pension is 55 for corporate pensions and 68 for state pensions. Every country's rules will differ, but I'll be writing about pension rules in the United Kingdom.

Some companies match for employee contributions. So if the employee contributes, for example, 5% through salary sacrifice, the company will match it with 5% based on your gross income, which is income before taxes are taken out. This is in effect free money from the company, and also from the state through not paying taxes on this amount.

Generally, to know what percentage of money you need to invest, divide your age by two. For example, if you are 20 years of age, you should be investing at 10%. You should also increase your percentage contribution when you get an income raise.

Pension fund companies grows these pensions by investing in bonds, stocks and shares, properties, and so on, so over time the pension grows by accumulating compound interest. Taxes eventually will be taken out, but only at the end through income drawdown.

Remember, any time you put away money to invest for your future, you are creating wealth and potentially generational wealth.

Life Insurance

If you have a mortgage and children, descendants, or people you love, you would hate to see them struggle when you are dead and gone. Consider having a life insurance policy and critical illness coverage to protect yourself—and those you care for. If you want to create generational wealth, having a life insurance in place will meant that at the time of your death, the insured amount will be paid out to the named dependants and automatically make them financially secure.

Some Life insurance with Critical illness built-in will pays out to you when you are terminally ill or pays out to your named dependants when you die. You pay premiums to receive a benefit at the end. Premiums are based on your current age, lifestyle (for instance, if you are a smoker or have any health issue), and how much coverage you want. Make sure all information you give to insurance companies is very accurate, because misrepresentations will be found out at the time of claim or payout.

Life insurance comes in many forms, including whole term, level term, and mortgage protection.

Whole life insurance protects the whole of your life because life is very unpredictable. Because of its unpredictability, premiums are very expensive. Whole life is more expensive because over the life of the policy, you are building up a cash reserve, and at some point you have paid the "whole" amount guaranteed by the policy. In certain countries, you are entitled to withdraw this amount, borrowing against yourself, or can leave it as a sort of savings account for the future. A whole life insurance is a good policy for building generational wealth.

Level term insurance pays a certain amount if you die within a set term. So you pay a monthly premium for a specific sum of money if the holder dies within a certain time of years. Term life is good only for as long as you are paying the monthly premiums, which increase as you age. It's cheaper because once you stop paying premiums, you get nothing—term life doesn't act like a savings account to build wealth. It's purely insurance rather than an investment that is guaranteed to pay out.

Then there is a mortgage-decreasing term assurance, which is set up in line with your mortgage so the amount of payout decreases as your mortgage decreases.

One thing to watch out for with mortgage insurance is whether it protects you or the bank. Mortgage loan insurance pays out to the bank in the event of your death, it ensures that the bank recoups the loan they gave you. To protect your heirs, you need the kind of insurance that pays off mortgage you owe on behalf of your heirs, so that they hold clear title.

You can insure for the amount you want, but you will pay the relevant premiums. Imagine having two children with an insurance policy that pays out £500,000 at the time of your death, instantly your children will be well off. If the insured amount is £1,000,000, then it's even better. Do not underestimate the power of a life insurance policy for building generational wealth.

The earlier you get life insurance in place, the better. But please choose the best, well-established companies with a good reputation in the insurance marketplace.

WRITING A WILL

If you are a parent and have a home, bank accounts, pension funds, insurance policies, land, properties, or businesses, then you need to write a will. This is how all that you have amassed during your lifetime will be passed on to the beneficiaries named on your will. If these beneficiaries are your own children or grandchildren, you are creating generational wealth.

Writing a will might sound scary to many as some people have a superstitious feeling that if they anticipate dying, it's somehow more likely to happen, but it will give you peace of mind. People often do not write a will because they assume their wealth will automatically go to their relatives. Some might think they are too young to write their will, or that they have not acquired anything worth writing into a will. Others worry that the process is going to be too complicated, very expensive, or boring.

Writing a will ensures that your preferences are enacted, but if you do not have a will and you die intestate, then state laws take effect. Depending on where you are and which country you live in, you may be able write your own will through a solicitor or you can also pick up a form at WH Smith for example to write your own will and this might be an inexpensive way to go. A Will simplifies the allocation of assets among your heirs or allows you to distribute assets according to how you perceive the needs of your heirs.

7

Using Credit

When you apply for credit, the lender will check your borrowing history and how you typically repay money you've borrowed. This happens when you apply for credit such as a loan, credit card, mortgage, car finance … even a mobile phone contract. They'll look at your credit history based on your credit report, which will show whether you have a mortgage, how much you owe on credit cards, and if you've missed payments in the past. This is combined with the other information you fill in on the credit application form and past information they've got on you (for example, if you're an existing customer). The lender will then decide if they'd like to lend you money.

Each lender uses slightly different lending criteria, so make sure you look around for a deal that's best suited to you—one you're more likely to be accepted for based on your credit history.

Your Credit Score

A credit score[9] is a number that reflects the likelihood of you paying credit back. Lenders like banks and credit card companies will look at your credit history when they calculate your credit score, which indicates the level of risk in lending to you. The higher your credit score, the better your chance of getting credit at the best rates.

Your credit score influences your chances of getting:

- credit cards, loans, and mortgages
- car financing
- gas and electricity monthly payments
- mobile phone contracts
- insurance paid monthly
- property rental

The Experian credit score runs from 0–999, based on the information in your Experian credit report. The higher your score, the greater the chance you have of getting the best credit deals.

Excellent (961–999). You should get the best credit cards, loans, and mortgages (but there are no guarantees).
Good (881–960). You should get most credit cards, loans, and mortgages, but may not be eligible for the very best deals.

---

[9] This chapter is adapted from the author's previous book, *From Debt to Wealth: Managing Personal Finance*, and is based on information on credit, credit reports, and credit scores taken from Experian, http://www.experian.co.uk/consumer/experian-credit-report.html.

Fair (721–880). You might get OK interest rates, but your credit limits may not be very high.

Poor (561–720). You might be accepted for credit cards, loans, and mortgages but they may have higher interest rates.

Very Poor (0–560). You're more likely to be rejected for most credit cards, loans, and mortgages.

Your Credit Report

A credit report details your personal credit history for accounts you've had in the last six years, including mortgages, credit cards, overdrafts, loans, mobile phone contracts, and even some utilities such as gas, electricity, and water. If you're over 18 and have taken out credit before, a credit reference agency is likely to hold a credit report on you.

A credit report gives lenders insight into your credit accounts, repayment records, and how well you're coping with your finances. Lenders usually have to tell you before they look at information from your credit report. They use it along with what you've provided on your application form and any information they might already have (if you're an existing customer) to help them decide whether or not to offer you credit—usually by calculating their own credit score for your application.

Your credit report contains the following kinds of information to help lenders confirm your identity and assess whether you're a reliable borrower.

Account information. A view of credit accounts you've had and whether you've made repayments on time and in full. Items such as missed or late payments stay on your credit report for at least six years, as do court judgments for non-payment of debts, bankruptcies, and individual voluntary arrangements.

Financial connections. A list of the people with whom you have a financial connection, such as a joint mortgage or bank account. These people are known as your financial associates. Their credit history doesn't appear in your credit report. However, when you apply for credit, lenders are able to look at their credit history also, as their circumstances could affect your ability to repay what you owe.

Address details. A view of electoral roll information for your current address and previous addresses you provide when you apply. Included are details of any other addresses you've been linked to in the past, such as those you've given to lenders on application forms.

The information in your credit report comes from two major sources.

Public information, including electoral roll information and court judgments.

Credit history information, information shared by lenders about what you owe and whether you've paid on time. You agree to this as part of any application for credit. Some lenders only contribute information on accounts that have defaulted, but these days most share monthly updates on all customers.

You should check your credit report if you're

- changing jobs or moving home
- applying for credit
- worried about ID fraud

Improving Your Credit Score

With a higher credit score, you've got a better chance of being accepted for credit at the best rates. So a high credit rating can mean you'll get a better deal on a credit card, a lower rate on a loan, and pay less interest on your mortgage. In other words, a high credit score can save you money.

So how do you get a good credit rating? Follow these twelve steps.

1. **Prove where you live.** Get on the electoral roll. This should be easy to do if you're a British or EU citizen. Lenders will check your name and address for proof that you live where you say you do. You can do this even if you are still living at home with parents, or sharing student accommodation. This makes it easier for banks and financial institutions to confirm your identity.
2. **Start to build credit history.** Having accounts such as a bank account can help. Initially, taking out a new account might see your score reduce a little, but managing it well should help to improve your Experian score whilst building your credit history. A bank account with an overdraft facility

is a form of credit and can show that you can keep within its spending limits.

3. **Have some responsible credit.** Lenders typically like to see a previous borrowing history. Taking out smaller forms of credit—such as a mobile phone contract, store card, or credit card—could make it easier to get accepted for major loans. If you manage the smaller forms of credit well, it show you know how to pay bills responsibly and on time each month.

4. **Consider closing unused accounts.** Consider closing unused credit accounts if you no longer require them. Lenders can take into account the credit limits available to you, not just what you currently owe. It could be better to have fewer, well-managed accounts and long-standing accounts with good histories.

5. **Space out credit applications.** Applying for lots of credit can suggest you are overly reliant on credit to supplement your income. If you can, aim for no more than one application for credit within a three month period. This could be applying for a credit card, debit card, mortgage, or car financing.

6. **Aim to have your credit accounts for a long time.** Having new credit account may result in a decrease to your Experian credit score. However, as your accounts get older, having multiple accounts which you are managing well could have a positive effect on your score.

7. **Aim to have a good amount of available credit.** Your 'available credit' is the difference between your

outstanding balance and your credit limit. If you have low available credit, or a large number of your accounts are using more than 50% of your available credit, banks and financial institutions may think you're struggling to manage your finances.

8. **Don't miss payments.** Any missed payments in the last six years will have a negative effect on your Experian credit score. As your late payments become older, they reduce the negative effect on your credit score.

9. **Avoid delinquent and defaulted accounts.** Accounts become delinquent when you're late on payment. Accounts are defaulted when the borrower fails to repay the loan as scheduled in the initial agreement. Defaulted accounts will drop off your credit report after six years, so long as they are satisfied.

10. **Avoid or resolve CCJs, IVAs or Scottish Trust Deeds.** A county court judgment (CCJ), bankruptcy, individual voluntary arrangement (IVA), or Scottish trust deed will have a negative effect on your Experian credit score for six years from the date the entry was recorded. These records should not appear on your credit report after six years as long as they have been settled or discharged.

11. **Protect your identity.** Look out for unfamiliar or suspicious entries in your report, such as an account you didn't open, a sudden surge in the amount you owe, or new credit applications you didn't make—they could mean you're a victim of identity fraud.

12. **Be aware of the effect of living abroad on your credit score.** If you have a credit history from a country where you resided previously, some lenders may be willing to take this into account when deciding whether to do business with you. You'll need to get a credit report from the credit reference agency in that country and share it with the lender, but it could be a big help.

Business Opportunities in Africa

As someone from an African background, I know that Africa offers many opportunities for investment compared to the rest of the world so I have discussed below some of the many opportunities available.

Agriculture

Globally, agriculture is big business, but not in Africa—even though the continent has about 60 per cent of the world's unused arable land with abundant labour resources and favourable climate in most parts. At the same time, we spend billions of dollars on food imports from other countries.

Farmers around the world may be rich, but in Africa farmers produce on a small scale, as production is more manual than mechanical, and they have limited capital or poor access to finance. So when we all pool monies to lend to these farmers through crowdfunding and then take a share of the profit at harvest time, that will boost food production, cut down on import costs, make profit for investors, and improve the economies and general wealth of African nations.

There are exciting trends unfolding before our eyes. A lot of people from countries such as the United States of America, China, Europe, India, and the Middle East are in search of business opportunities that are not crude oil, mineral resources, or commodities. Many foreign investors understand that there is a lot of money to be made in Africa. There are also new trends within Africa to solve Africa's unique problems.

Here are some crowdfunding companies trying to solve Africa's farming problems.

Ghana
AgricGH - https://allagricgh.com/?
Agripool
Farmable World Company Ltd
Grow For Me, https://www.growforme.com/en
Complete Farmer, https://www.completefarmer.com

Nigeria
Farm Crowding, https://www.farmcrowdy.com/#/
Thrive Agric, https://www.thriveagric.com

Somalia
RE Farming

South Africa
Livestock Wealth, https://livestockwealth.com

Local Products

Branding local products for export adds value to the products and takes advantage of the international market. Every year, Africa spends billions of money on imports, including both food and non-food items. But beyond the traditional commodities such as minerals, crude oil, cocoa, African coffee, and timber, there are many products on the continent of Africa with the potential to become global brands. While we often look down on them, a few interesting entrepreneurs are turning these products into bestsellers, focusing on organic products to add value and bring a premium price. Examples turning cocoa into chocolates, or shea butter into beauty and skin care products.

Affordable Housing

Many people in Africa don't have a place to live. As people move into big cities, urbanisation is creating housing shortages. Good business opportunities are to build affordable housing and estate housing, and cement production. Some entrepreneurs are turning decommissioned shipping containers into cheap housing.

Aliko Dangote has long been producing cement for the African continent, and more recently Ibrahim Mahama of Ghana has been producing Dzata cement, but more is needed. Africa is a big continent and is still under-producing on all levels. Setting yourself up in the cement and housing sector is sure be big business, as the housing deficit is big. Nigeria alone has a housing deficit of about 20 million homes, and South Africa a deficit of 2.3 million homes. Africa's housing crisis opens a great opportunities for entrepreneurs.

Virtual Education

There is a trend of academic inflation happening all over Africa. To compete for job opportunities, Africans are embarking on academic degrees and programs for employment prospects, with flexible learning and cheap fees helping to make their CVs look impressive and to allow them to better themselves through career progression and promotions at work. With the help of computers and the internet, online courses are booming, opening up new opportunities for education.

If you are a teacher or an educational institution looking to expand your market, focus on Africa. You can partner with universities abroad for academic degrees. Even higher education can be attained through virtual universities.

Low-Cost Private Schools

It is estimated that one in four African students will be enrolled in private schools, since most of the public schools have been neglected and are underperforming. Therefore starting a private school as a way to make money helps to build generational wealth. Having great infrastructure, great teachers, and fantastic curriculum with affordable school fees is the way to go.

Outsourcing

Business process outsourcing now offers huge business opportunities in Africa. The rising dominance of e-commerce and the digital economy is leading companies to demand more data and real-time services across multiple platforms. More companies are outsourcing their data processing needs, customer services, human talent, supply chain needs, and accountancy to Africa. India and the Philippines have already benefited from outsourcing, but the opportunities are growing in Africa.

There are English, French, and Spanish speakers in Africa, so neither language nor internet services would be a barrier to doing business there. And besides, it's cheap to run such businesses in Africa.

Fashion Industry

Fashion is a more than $2.4 trillion dollar industry globally which uses cotton, silk, and fibres. Even though cotton, silk, and fibres are all produced in Africa, Africans are not really taking advantage of this booming industry through branding of clothes and apparel. Hence, Africa owns only a thin slice of the global fashion industry.

The global fashion industry has a vast and complex value chain that stretches from the farmers who grow the cotton, silk, and fibres to the factories in Asia that spin the fibres into textiles, and then to the garment factories that convert the textiles into apparel sold in shops in London, New York, Milan, Paris, and Dubai.

Thankfully, African entrepreneurs are catching up with other creative entrepreneurs globally to be included in this value chain. Africa has a high population coupled with cheap labour and raw materials, so building a fashion industry in Africa can be big business.

The African Development Bank estimates the African fashion industry to be about $15.5 billion over five years, so taking advantage of opportunities now is important.

Urban Logistics

Most cities in Africa have not diversified the transport system, and as more and more people flow into the city over the next ten to twenty years, transportation needs will multiply enormously. Already, about sixty African cities have a population of over a million. Congestion is one of the biggest problems in Africa and still growing, so getting around a city can be a challenge. It is a logistics nightmare that worries both businesses and consumers.

However, some entrepreneurs in Africa are already taking advantage of the challenge by setting up businesses that use technologies to serve customers, for example by taking orders and delivering food or shopping directly to their location. Their clients avoid driving to the market to create further chaos in traffic, and the entrepreneurs boost their businesses.

The future of Africa lies with such entrepreneurs, and there are more opportunities now than ever in Africa so it is important to instil entrepreneurship in your children and positioning the next generation to participate in future prosperity in Africa.

Fintech Industry

It's not surprising that there is a gold rush in Africa within the financial technology or 'fintech' industry, and a few people know this. Digital financial services are attracting more investors in Africa than any other business. More people now have access to the internet, computers, and mobile phones. However, over 60 per cent of the adult population in Africa are unbanked, and this remains a huge market for financial services.

By using mobile phone technologies and the internet, fintech industries across the African continent are able to reach customers, deepening their financial inclusion and offering incredible opportunities by offering them financial services through processing payments, money transfers, and access to credit and savings. It is projected that in the next three to ten years, fintech industries will see growth in the billions and contribute at least 200 billion in US dollars to the GDP of Africa. This is why many fintech industries are rushing into Africa to take advantage of this booming industry.

According to Fintechnews.africa, between the first and third quarters of 2021, Africa fintech companies raised USD 1.44 billion in funding, an amount expected to increase annually for start-ups and growth. Eight companies have caught the attention of global investors like Softbank, Sequoia, Founders Fund, Ribbit Capital, and Tiger Global.

1. **Opay** from Nigeria
2. **Wave** from Senegal
3. **Chipper Cash** in California, which operates in six African countries as well as in the UK and US as a money transfer company, offering also digital card, stock, and crypto investing
4. **Flutterwave**, which is headquartered in California but has a presence in twelve African countries in addition to operating in Europe and the US markets
5. **MNT-Halan**, headquartered in Egypt, which provides consumer lending such as Nano loans, payroll lending, digital payments
6. **Tala**, headquartered in California, providing digital consumer credit micro-loans of USD 10 to USD 500.
7. **Jumo**, a South African company that provides the core banking infrastructure such as Know Your Customer (KYC), underwriting, fraud detection solutions, amongst others
8. **MFS** from South Africa, which provides digital payments between borders and currencies—mobile money wallets and cross-border payments.

The fintech industry is lucrative and booming in Africa, so if you have an interest in this sector, research and start your own Fintech Industry.

Off-Grid Solar

Africa has abundant sunshine and a demand for solar energy. People are tired of the centrally managed power grid that is poorly managed, slow to deploy, inefficient, inflexible, and unable to meet their energy needs. The continent enjoys over 300 days of sunshine annually, and solar entrepreneurs will prosper in this sector of renewable energy.

The World Bank's climate action fund of USD 200 billion is available to tap into. Shell also has a budget for clean energy that can be accessed by entrepreneurs in the solar business.

Waste

If you've been to a few African countries, you have seen a lot of waste that is not being managed properly. Fortunately, there is millions of dollars to be made in this business. The investment you need in this sector is pick-up trucks, dumping locations, and human capital.

Tourism

There has been a lot of interest in Africa in investment for purely travel. A lot of people, for example African Americans who think of going back to Africa or tourists who feel they've travelled too much in the West, would like to explore Africa. Agri-tourism, wellness tourism, and cultural tours are all business opportunities.

A tour guide company can be built around such events as The Year of Return or festivals such as Afrochela in

Ghana and other African countries. There are lucrative opportunities waiting to be explored further.

Wellness Tourism

With the middle class increasing in numbers in Africa and people being more careful about with what they eat and put on, coupled with the advantage of Africa having all the natural resources for products such as cosmetics, getting into the wellness business should not be a challenge at all, once better strategies and good marketing are put in place.

On the service side, you can have a spa or offer massage, and even coaching on healthy eating. On the product side, you can consider cosmetics.

Build a brand, not a commodity. Make sure the experience is great. Your product should tell a story that people can be affiliated with.

Side Hustles

If your income falls short of your expectations, you can try to increase it by renegotiating your pay. But if that pay raise isn't enough or doesn't come through, start a side hustle.

Following are some ideas on the market. If you are not doing these already but have the passion to venture into one or two, start now and see where destiny might take you.

YouTube. You can receive income by running a program on YouTube. Revenue is paid through adverts, but you need an internet connection.

TikTok. This new creative way to make money is as easy as showcasing your talent to attract viewers.[10]

Offer a course. Membership sites such as Thinkific and Udemy give you the opportunity to run a course. You receive monthly income or regular income. The course is created once, but sells regularly.

Digital products. E-books are created once but give you a consistent income through royalties and fees. Digital products can be bought online twenty-four hours a day, 365 days a year.

Affiliate marketing. This is commission-based marketing to promote someone else's business and products. You make money when someone purchases the product from your link and you earn commission. Research if you are interested.

Blogging. Monetise your blog through adverts via Google, Facebook, Twitter, Instagram, and other social media. The challenge is to focus on quality and consistency.

Social media managing. If you've been successful with your own online platforms, use those skills and get paid to nanaging other people's social media.

Rentals and buy-to-let properties. Rent out your spare room if you have one. Invest in buy-to-let properties if you can, as these are good for cash flow. You can even buy a property to flip it.

E-commerce. You can sell merchandise through online stores, like Etsy.

---

[10] For tips, see Joseph Todd, 'Monetize Your TikTok Account (7 Ways To Make $1000)', YouTube video, https://www.youtube.com/watch?v=VXKrXNE-2B4.

Drop shipping. The wholesaler ships products on your behalf to the customer.

Ebay. Selling stuff you don't need can be very lucrative.

Freelancing. Bookkeeping, copy writing, editing, and book writing allow you to use specific skills to earn extra income.

Coaching and speaking engagements. Get paid for sharing your interests, passions, and talents.

Families Who Have Created Generational Wealth

Building a legacy is not always about passing on money. It's also about leadership, leaving a good name, knowledge, a family mission and values, traditions and memories, the family council, learning and growing together, serving and nurturing people, investing in human capital, and other less tangible goods. Someone can win the lottery today, and in a year's time be unable to account for the money because they did not have the qualities to manage their wealth—this ability was never instilled in them from their younger years. This tells you that when it comes to money, even though it is important, other life's qualities are more important in order to grow. I am therefore sharing the below famous family histories of achievement and successes to inspire readers to start their own family legacy.

Nelson Mandela

Nelson Mandela was an anti-apartheid activist and the first black president of South Africa. He was born 18 July 1918 in Mvezo, a descendant of the Thembu royal family. Mandela's father served as the local chief and councillor, and after the death of his father, Nelson was brought to the Thembu monarchy to be raised by the chief's regent. Living among the royal family exposed Mr Mandela to powerful examples of leadership that remained models for him throughout his life.

Mandela studied law at the university in Johannesburg. He was a frequent target of racism, as he was the only black student in the school, and he decided to enrol himself into radical politics. In 1944, Mandela joined the African National Congress (ANC), an anti-colonialist political party that sought to empower the black people in government, wealth, land acquisition and ownership, equal opportunities, equal human rights, more work, and security. To Mr Mandela, South Africa belonged to both blacks and whites, and every decision made should be for the benefit of the people and not under oppression.

Within the ANC, Mandela quickly rose in ranks with Walter Sisulu and Oliver Thambo. With the ANCs rise to power in 1948, South Africa's racial inequality was highlighted, and the Government passed legislation that institutionalised discrimination and enforced the supremacy of the minority white population. Mandela and the ANC fought back, launching the Defiance Campaign in 1952, a series of nonviolent actions uniting black, Indian, and communist coalitions who coordinated civil disobedience. The national party cracked down on their efforts, and after a series of events, and in 1962, Mandela was captured. He received a life sentence and was incarcerated at Robben Island. With Mandela in jail, the campaign died out.

But Nelson Mandela did not give up whilst in prison. He continued to fight on a smaller scale, fighting against the prison's inhuman conditions through demonstrations and teachings. Calls for Mandela's freedom began to build global support, and finally, in 1990 after twenty-seven years, Mr Mandela was released from prison. South Africa conducted its first open elections in 1994, and Mandela became president.

In order to be able to instil the kind of strength and qualities shown by Mandela in your descendants, you have to have had it yourself, because you cannot teach what you do not know. Better start learning to better yourself so your knowledge and discipline can be passed on to your generations. Demonstrate discipline and responsibility yourself, evaluate and advocate for the less privileged, participate in planning and making decisions for the disadvantaged, and mentor other family members and anyone you come across, in effect building and leaving a good name.

Generational wealth is not all about money, but leadership and building a legacy. Mandela indeed built a legacy of leadership, tolerance, and freedom for his people.

The Walton Family

The Waltons are America's richest family, owning Walmart retail shops in Argentina, Brazil, Canada, Chile, China, and Mexico; Asda and its associated businesses in the United Kingdom; Massmart in Botswana, Kenya, Malawi, Mauritius, Mozambique, Namibia, Nicaragua, Nigeria, South Africa, Swaziland, Tanzania, Uganda, Zambia and Ghana; Seiyu Group in Japan; Flipkart Private Limited in

India; the membership-only Sam's Club; the Walton Family Foundation, and many more.[11]

Sam Walton was an American businessman and entrepreneur who was the founder of the Walmart retail shops. Walmart, founded in 1962 and taken public in 1970, today is the biggest business according to revenue in the United States.[12]

Sam Walton's vision was to reduce the cost of living for everyone who shopped in his shop. His secret was working together with his family and employees—he built his company on people. He believed the success they had was because of their people. He made partners of their employees, and has been sincere and shared profits with them, and they have worked hard in turn. They've kept their prices lower than their competitors. Sam treated everybody as equals, because in his mind, we are all created by one Maker. He treated his employees and workers no different from how he would treat the president of the United States. Sam viewed his role in the company as being the person who showed respect to everybody. Sam liked taking risks and gambling on new strategies. He was always driven by his vision of reducing the cost of living for his community and for all.

Sam Walton and his wife, Helen, together had four children, Rob, John, Jim, and Alice. Rob took over the

---

[11] Wikipedia, s.v. 'List of assets owned by Walmart', https://en.wikipedia.org/wiki/List_of_assets_owned_by_Walmart; Tom Metcalf, 'These Are the World's Richest Families', Bloomberg (1 August 2020), https://www.bloomberg.com/features/richest-families-in-the-world.

[12] 'Profile: Walton Family', Forbes, https://www.forbes.com/profile/walton-1/?sh=eb95f756f3f8.

family business as chairman after their father's death, whilst John served as a director before he died in a plane crash in the mid-2000s. Jim and Alice are not directly involved in the business, but Jim's son Steuart is fully on board.

According to Bloomberg and the *Mirror* newspaper in the UK, the Walton family business grows at a whopping £57,000 every minute, £3.3 million every hour, and £82 million every day.[13] In January 2020, Investopedia put their year-end revenue to $524 billion and consolidated income of $14.9 billion.[14]

The Rothschild Family

Mayer Amschel Rothschild was born in 1744 to Jewish parents who lived in Germany. He learnt about the business world at quite an early stage in his life. His father, Amschel Moses Rothschild, used to trade coins and other commodities for a living. Mayer became an orphan when both his parents died of smallpox and had to fend for himself. At age 13, he took an apprenticeship with a Hanover banking firm in Germany and learned the ins and outs of banking and foreign trade from bankers who used their extensive connections and skills to serve the reigning

---

[13] Ben Weich, 'Inside World's Wealthiest Family—Who Earn a Whopping £57,000 Every Minute', *Mirror* (17 August 2019), updated 18 August 2019, accessed 13 December 2020.

[14] Nathan Reiff, '5 Companies Owned by Walmart', Investopedia (7 April 2020), https://www.investopedia.com/articles/markets/102315/top-4-companies-owned-walmart.asp.

nobility. Some of these bankers had risen to the status of what was known as the '"court Jews" or court factors'.[15]

At age 19, Mayer Amschel Rothschild returned to his hometown in Frankfurt and along with his brothers continued to trade in the commodities and rare coins business their father had engaged in, together with the money-trading business. Through his rare coins business, he met Crown Prince Wilhelm, who in 1785 became Wilhelm IX, Landgrave of Hesse-Kassel, and eventually the European continent's richest man. Rothschild soon started providing other banking services to Wilhelm and a number of nobles. By the year 1769, he was given the title of court factor. He married in 1770 and went on to have ten children, five boys and five girls.

Expanding and Controlling the Rothschild Footprint

The Rothschild banking empire benefited tremendously from the French Revolution. During the war, Rothschild facilitated monetary transactions for Hessian mercenary soldiers.

Around that same time, Rothschild sent his sons to live in the capital cities of various European countries with the goal of establishing banking businesses in Naples, Vienna, Paris, and London, in addition to Frankfurt. With Mayer Rothschild's children spread across Europe, the five linked branches became, in effect, the first bank to transcend borders.

---

[15] This account of the Rothschild family is taken from Jennifer Cook, 'A History of the Rothschild Family', Investopedia (updated 11 June 2021), https://www.investopedia.com/updates/history-rothschild-family/

Lending to governments to finance war operations over several centuries provided the Rothschild family with ample opportunity to accumulate bonds and build additional wealth in a range of different industries.

Before he died in 1812, Mayer Rothschild left strict rules for his descendants on how they should handle the family's finances. He wanted to keep the fortune within the family and, as such, encouraged the arrangement of marriages among relatives. According to an article published in the August 2003 issue of Discover magazine entitled "Go Ahead, Kiss Your Cousin," Mayer Amschel Rothschild arranged his affairs so that cousin marriages among his descendants were inevitable.

His will barred female descendants from any direct inheritance. Without an inheritance, female Rothschilds had few possible marriage partners of the same religion and suitable economic and social stature, except other Rothschilds. Rothschild brides bound the family together. Four of Mayer's granddaughters married grandsons, and one married her uncle. These were hardly people whose mate choice was limited by the distance they could walk on their day off.

From Jennifer Cook, 'A History of the Rothschild Family', Investopedia (updated 11 June 2021), https://www.investopedia.com/updates/history-rothschild-family.

Of Mayer Rothschild's four sons, the third, Nathan (1777–1836), achieved the greatest success. Nathan took over the lead role in pioneering international finance.

Nathan moved to England in 1798. There he founded a textile jobbing business with £20,000 of working capital, the equivalent of £2 million today. He eventually founded a bank, which became N M Rothschild & Sons Ltd. Although privately held and still controlled by the Rothschild family, in 2015 N M Rothschild & Sons Ltd. reported a net income of £51.558 million.

Like the other Rothschild banks that were subsequently set up throughout Europe, N M Rothschild & Sons Ltd. furnished credit to the government during times of war and crisis. During the Napoleonic Wars, for example, it managed and financed various subsidies the British government sent to its different allies and lent funds to pay the British troops, almost single-handedly financing the British war effort.

In 1824, Nathan Rothschild and Moses Montefiore cofounded the Alliance Assurance Company, which lives on today as RSA Insurance Group. Nathan also gained the rights to the Almadén mines from the Spanish government in 1835, securing a European monopoly on mercury, which was used to refine gold and silver. The supply of the chemical came in handy in the 1850s when N M Rothschild & Sons started to refine gold and silver for the Bank of England and the Royal Mint.

Nathan contributed to many areas of philanthropy in the Jewish community. His family later expanded these charitable efforts to other populations in Paris and London. His earliest efforts went toward synagogues in London. He continued to champion this work, which eventually led to the formation of the United Synagogue, a larger organization that helped streamline the causes of the smaller individual synagogues. Later, various family members supported the creation of Israel and helped with the construction of government buildings.

Rothschild had seven children with his wife, Hannah Barent Cohen. Those children followed and built on their family's philanthropic tradition. The Rothschild Archive reports that Nathan's youngest child, Louise, and her seven daughters took responsibility for many of the thirty

Rothschild charitable foundations in Frankfurt. These foundations included public libraries, orphanages, hospitals, homes for the elderly, and special funds allocated for the purpose of education.

The Jews' Free School in London, in particular, received extensive financial support. Educational efforts in Austria, France, and Israel were also made possible through Rothschild generosity. In addition to monies put toward education, the family gave an estimated 60,000 pieces of artwork to numerous organizations. The Rothschild family expanded the creation of social housing in the cities of London and Paris, and the Rothschild Foundation was created to further these efforts.

Today, the Rothschild family build their wealth through financial services, real estate, energy, mining, charitable work, and wineries in North America, South America, South Africa, Europe, and Australia. The fortune of the Rothschilds is held in family corporations, and most family members are directly employed by these corporations. The family's success is due to their strong unity and interest in cooperation such as entrepreneurship and their smart business principles.

The family's Latin motto is *Concordia, Integritas, Industria*, which means ‹Harmony, Integrity, Industry'.

The Rockefellers

The Rockefeller family traces their wealth to their founding father, John D, Davison Rockefeller Snr, who started Standard Oil in 1870. Standard Oil grew to control most of the oil-refining companies in the United States, making

John the richest man in the nation and the country's first billionaire. Rockefeller's business and wealth grew with the demand for kerosene and gasoline as oil was used throughout the country before the emergence of electricity, eventually giving him control of 90% of all oil in the US.[16]

In order to break this monopoly of the oil industry, the Supreme Court in 1911 ruled against Standard Oil for violating federal antitrust laws. It was then divided into thirty-four separate entities, which became the Chevron Corporation, ExxonMobil, and others. Later, it was realised that the individual companies were worth even more than the single company before it was broken up. Shares were doubled and tripled in their early years, eventually making Rockefeller the country's first billionaire, with a fortune equivalent to nearly 2% of the whole of the US national economy.

John spent the last forty years of his life in retirement in New York. His fortune is used for philanthropic work in medicine, education, and science research. Rockefeller founded the University of Chicago, Rockefeller University, Central Philippines University in the Philippines, the Rockefeller Foundation, and the General Education Board. John was a devout Baptist and supported a lot of churches, abstained from alcohol and tobacco, and relied heavily on the advice of his wife, Laura Spelman Rockefeller, with whom he had five children, Bessie, Alice, Alta Edith, and John Jnr. He was a very faithful father, husband, and congregant at the Erie Street Baptist Church, where he taught Sunday

---

[16] Rockefeller Archive Center, https://rockarch.org/resources/about-the-rockefellers; Wikipedia, s.v. John D. Rockefeller', https://en.wikipedia.org/wiki/John_D._Rockefeller.

school and served as a trustee, clerk, and occasional janitor. John believed religion to be the source of his wealth and success. He stated that 'from the beginning, I was trained to work, save and to give'. John's friends described him as reserved, earnest, religious, methodical, and discreet. He was an excellent debater and well spoken, with deep love for music.

The Dangote Family

According to Forbes.com, Aliko Dangote is the richest man in Africa, with a net worth of $10.1 billion, dealing originally in cement, sugar, and flour within Africa and now oil and gas too. Aliko Dangote is from a wealthy family, headed by his wealthy father Mohammed Dangote and his mother Mary Dantata, who is the granddaughter of Alhassan Dantata, a famous businessman who in his time was the richest man in Africa. Aliko Dangote was raised by his maternal family and schooled in Kano. He later obtained his bachelor's of science in business administration from Al-Azhar University in Egypt.[17]

He was born on 10 April 1957 in the city of Kano in Kano State. He had an entrepreneurial mindset from his early years. In primary school, he would buy cartons of sweets and resell them to his classmates, making him money. In 1977, at the age of 21, he started out by establishing a small

---

[17] 'Aliko Dangote – Family, Family Tree', CelebFamily, https://www.celebfamily.com/entrepreneur/aliko-dangote-family.html; Ndaba Lungu, 'Most Affluent Families In Africa That You Probably Never Knew About', Africa.com (8 January 2020), https://africa.com/most-affluent-families

business in Kano as the Dangote Group. His start-up was funded by his late uncle, Sanusi Dantata. He later relocated his business to Lagos, and today it is the biggest business in Africa, worth trillions of Nigerian naira and billions in US dollars.

Aliko Dangote owns 85% of the publicly traded Dangote Cement through a holding company.[18] Dangote cement operates in ten African countries and produces 45.6 million metric tons annually. He also owns stakes in other publicly traded sugar and salt manufacturing companies. Since 2016, he has been constructing one of the biggest oil refinery in Nigeria that will be one of the world's largest oil refineries once it's completed.

Aliko Dangote comes from a third-generation wealthy family dynasty which started from his grandfather and passed to his father and then to him.[19] Both his parents came from wealthy homes and passed down their wealth and knowledge to their descendants. That's the beauty of generational wealth.

The Kenyatta Family

Jomo Kenyatta, born Kamau Ngengi, is known as the founding father of Kenya. He was the leader of the Kenyan Independence Movement and Kenya's first prime minister as well as president. He is known in Kenya as the equivalent of

---

[18] 'Profile: Aliko Dangote', Forbes, https://www.forbes.com/profile/aliko-dangote/?list=africa-billionaires&sh=1513642f22fc

[19] Anina Visser, 'Meet the 5 Richest Families in Africa', Business Insider South Africa (20 August 2018), https://www.businessinsider.co.za/meet-the-5-richest-families-in-africa-2018-8

Thomas Jefferson, Ben Franklin, and Paul Revere all rolled into one, but particularly he was the Kenyan.

Jomo Kenyatta was from the Kikuyu tribe. He was born in the 1890s but his exact date of birth is not known, as his tribe did not keep track of birthdates and calendar years. As a young boy, Jomo Kenyatta was fascinated by the world beyond his village and later ran away from home, joined the church of Scotland Mission, and received his basic education. He received his baptism as Johnstone Kamau in 1914, left the mission, and went to Nairobi, which led to the influx of the Kikuyu youth to the cities. Whilst in Nairobi, he adopted the name Kenyatta, being a term for the belt he wore. He worked his way into a post on the town council, got married, and started his family.

Whilst in Nairobi, Kenyatta was introduced to the East Africa Association, a protest movement against the white European government that had transformed Kenya into a British colony and seized a big amount of Kikuyu lands. He became heavily involved in the organisation, later renamed the Kikuyu Central Association (KCA). He travelled to London on behalf of KCA in 1929 to protest against British plans to combine Kenya, Uganda, and Tanganyika.

Throughout the 1930s and 1940s, he travelled extensively, studied, and wrote, eventually becoming a leading figure in Kikuyu and African rights in Kenya.

> He helped articulate the goals of the KCA to the British people through editorials and lectures, he generated an academic awareness of Kikuyu issues through his book *Facing Mount Kenya*, and he helped

organize the fifth Pan-African Congress, chaired by W.E.B. Du Bois, to encourage cooperation between black Africans under white rule. In this time, he adopted the name *Jomo*, which meant Burning Spear. In these years, Jomo Kenyatta was really born as a major political figure.

In 1946 when he was back in Kenya, he became the president of Kenyan African Union whose aim was to fight politically for independence and in In 1952 a series of Kikuyu groups started a very violent uprising against the British called the Mau Mau rebellion. Although Kenyatta was not involved in this movement, he was arrested. Nevertheless, in the 1950s and 1960s the world was changing. Britain was facing major pressure to decolonize most of its remaining empire and started preparing Kenya for self-rule. Kenyan nationalists formed their own political party, the Kenya African National Union, and elected Kenyatta the president, despite his still being imprisoned.

Kenyatta reassured the anxious nation by claiming that Europeans should be allowed to live peacefully alongside Africans as equals, and in 1961 he was released from prison. Finally, in 1962, Kenyatta was invited to the London Conference to negotiate the constitutional terms of

Kenyan independence. On December 12, 1963, Kenya celebrated its independence with Jomo Kenyatta as its prime minister. That title was changed to president a year later.[20]

This was the beginning of their presidential legacy.

It is important not only to focus on building assets for our generations but also help build leadership qualities into our children and children's children like these families have done.

---

[20] 'Jomo Kenyatta: Biography & Facts', Study.com (7 August 2022), https://study.com/academy/lesson/jomo-kenyatta-biography-facts.html.

Conclusion

If you have not started building wealth already, there is no better time than now. Here are my parting tips.

- Avoid consumer debt, and save more money.
- Work hard, either by having a job you go to or building your own businesses or side hustles.
- Be a forward thinker and strategic in everything you plan to do, including owning assets.
- Diversify your income into different types of assets.
- If possible, make sure you have your pensions in place, whether a state pension, corporate, or private.
- A life insurance policy is also very important. Make sure you have one in place, together with a written will.

When all is well, start supporting others. It is better to give than to receive, and charity makes you have a mentality of abundance. Generational wealth is not all about money but also about family unity, support, and teaching and learning together in everything you do.

Resources

SIDE HUSTLES
https://www.freelancer.co.uk

https://www.peopleperhour.com

https://www.betterteam.com/uk/peopleperhour

https://www.upwork.com

https://www.fiverr.com

INVESTMENT PLATFORMS
https://www.hl.co.uk

https://www.ajbell.co.uk

https://www.vanguardinvestor.co.uk

https://www.barclays.co.uk/smart-investor/

https://www.fidelity.co.uk

https://m1.com/how-it-works/invest/

https://us.etrade.com/home

https://www.schwab.com

https://www.forbes.com/sites/dennisjaffe/2020/04/15/how-wealthy-families-develop-new-family-leaders-a-program-that-empowers-next-generation-stewards/?sh=6567748b6095

https://www.forbes.com/sites/deloitte/2020/11/04/the-value-of-resilient-leadership/?sh=586b68076d11

https://medium.com/@mary_agbesanwa/14-lessons-on-building-generational-wealth-for-millennials-585d6360b6bf

https://www.bloomberg.com/features/richest-families-in-the-world/

https://en.wikipedia.org/wiki/Jomo_Kenyatta

https://www.britannica.com/biography/Uhuru-Kenyatta

CLIENT TESTIMONIALS FOR FINANCIAL COACHING BY THE AUTHOR

To book for financial coaching, you can reach out to the author through her website: https://www.maryayisi.com

Pamela
It was a pleasure first seeing a black woman with such a wealth of information and willing to share it with others. May GOD restore you and may you never lack in any area of your life, your husband's life and your children, children's children's. Generational wealth is one of your giftings, and I am honored to get these services and I respect you and your time.

Thank you

Noks
It has been an "eye opener" and extremely educational working with Eagle Mary. She explains concepts in a way that Kingdom Citizens understand where and how they need to take action. I have already started implementing what I have been taught and cannot wait to learn more and make the necessary changes to ensure I secure that Generational Wealth that will be my legacy to my children and generations to come. Thank you Eagle Mary for allowing God to use you in this powerful way to guide Kingdom Citizens on how to manage and build on their finances

Devadanam
I'm very glad have you as my Coach in times like this. I like your passion for coaching us. It's subjective, very useful and needed nowadays. With two sessions i learnt so much.

And waiting for other sessions. After finishing the sessions i may get full subject. Thank you very much. Thankful to our Coach. And first of all all Glory to God.

Lize

It's a great honor to e-meet you and have a very productive session.

Thank you so much.

Catherine

I went over and above the budget, I also realized that I need to build an emergency fund as I do not have one. Tracking my expenses, made me hesitate in doing some impromptu purchases.

Josiah

Good morning Eagle Mary, thank you so much for all the valuable financial management tips you are sharing with me. I feel encouraged and motivated to implement every bit of advice you have given to me knowing the benefits of paying off the debt and being free. God bless you so much for all your work in helping us in Jesus's name.

Nyazema

It has been an "eye opener" and extremely educational working with Eagle Mary. She explains concepts in a way that Kingdom Citizens understand where and how they need to take action. I have already started implementing what I have been taught and cannot wait to learn more and make the necessary changes to ensure I secure that Generational Wealth that will be my legacy to my children and generations to come. Thank you Eagle Mary for allowing

God to use you in this powerful way to guide Kingdom Citizens on how to manage and build on their finances

Josiah
Reading the book while taking the 1 on 1 lesson is a transformational experience. The book is a convenient summary of all the handy tips you need to know about building generational wealth while the lessons provide you with a rare opportunity to build a working plan for managing your personal finances with the essential guidance of Coach Mary. I feel confident about getting rid of my pecuniary worries by practicing all that I have learned.

Catherine
I have come to appreciate the fact that I need to be deliberate in my finances. The approach she used during the sessions really hit home. The practical application of the sessions has enabled me to identify places I need to make changes. My finances have started to make sense. It's clear to me now what I need to do to build my wealth. Thank you for this eye opening experience.

Kuda
One of the things you are never taught at most schools is the management of your own finances. The course was an eye opener well thought out and designed to equip you for the future . I did pray the prayers to get out of debt a few years ago and managed to get rid of it. The debt fleetly reappeared as i had no robust system in place of managing my personal finances. After this course with Coach Mary I am confident debt will not be my portion ever again as I am managing my finances effectively. Thank you Coach.

William

This is very rewarding to me, I have for the first time richly appreciated the mutual funds and other kinds of investments as the enlightenment by the Coach is making me relate with facts on the ground very well.